REFLECTIONS AT VARIOUS SPEEDS

Christopher Michael Carter

Supposed Crimes LLC • Matthews, North Carolina

This book is a work of fiction. Names, characters, places, and incidents are products of the author's imagination or are used fictitiously. Any resemblance to actual events or locales or persons, living or dead, is entirely coincidental.

All Rights Reserved
Copyright © 2017 Christopher Michael Carter

Published in the United States.

ISBN: 978-1-944591-46-5

www.supposedcrimes.com

This book is typeset in Goudy Old Style.

Much of this collection is comprised of lyrics written from when I was but a young lad (teenager and slightly over) with aspirations and delusions of becoming a singer/songwriter/rock star/what have you, long before Gun Control for Polar Bears was written with a few pieces that were written afterwards. I still play music today but I much prefer instrumental pieces. Eventually I'll record and release the various pieces I've been tooling around with for some time. For now, enjoy the words of yesteryear along with various pieces written between then and now.
- Christopher

Persistence (and the Blood on My Hands)
I know the secrets
You aren't lying anymore
I need the reasons
Ethic's at the door
Thrown in my face
Forget the problem filled past
And steady the pace
Well I know the shadows bleed
You wouldn't understand
It's the blood on my hands
All this time, never clean
Time is watching
Waiting so patiently for me to give up so easily
But I won't give up, I must survive the tide
But do I have the strength to give it a go?
Do I have the strength to let this flow?
Do I have the strength to carry this on?
What if I fail?
Will I be missed when I'm gone?
Do I have the strength?
Let me know
All I need is someone to comfort me
All I want is someone to hold on to
And all I...
All I need is someone else to question why
Why do we live these troubled lives?
And all I...
I'm not going to change my life this way
I've grown with what I have today
No, it's not perfect
It's what I've had to cope with
I can't back out of it
I won't back down
No, not today
Not today

Scatter
Don't let them take your soul away
Clouding the blue-lit day
Lingering as death at my door
Scatter, scatter
I just turn away
And vanish in the day
And let them all say what they want to say

Dark Halo
Fat force of dream
Darkness is a vision
A vision you cannot see
Light from the television
Blinds you so easily
Full force of stream
Light is a reflection
Of a shadow's other side
Shielding from neglect
Spread your wings and glide
Such a dark halo
Atop such a sweet sorrow

The Escapist
So daring, you want to jump
Yet so selfish you want to live
So stupid to take it all away

Everything's Alright
The tie that binds
The road that winds
Around your heart and through your mind
You're dragging me down
I can feel it
No, don't try
You can't keep it
Why does love always end in goodbye?
Why can't we see things eye to eye?
You're taking my heart
I can't feel it
No, no don't try to kill it
Don't want to have to say goodnight
Can't we just say everything's alright?

Just Me

Cutting deeper every time
I look in the mirror and I find
It won't go, go away - it's just me
Wish I wasn't cursed
Feeling rage, I would burst
But I know my hands are tied
I would express my fear in large strides
You wear your smile
Ear to ear
I stuffed too much down to let it go
Right behind me every time like a shadow
Still can't believe it follows me
Even when I swerve quickly
I see
The fear will never leave
Into the dark I fade out
Swallowed by the pitch black ground
Locked away from my own fear
A fear that gets so much worse from here
I try my best to spit this out
Always seems so different coming out of my mouth
Put myself down with jealousy
Can't even see past my own pity
I try to lead my life
Bad thoughts are always with me
I can't seem to say what I mean
I try to walk my paths
Bad vibes cloud me blindly
I can never tell just what you say
Can't shake what follows me
Everything seems so close behind
And all I know is that I can't change it all
Just a matter of time
And time is all I need to sit back and watch it all fall

Never Again
Can you feel?
I can't deal
What is real?
Please tell me
I'm trying to die
I can't feel you
I'm dying to try
I can't feel you
Never again
Will we speak
My friend
And never again
Will we cry
Never again
Will this leak
My friend
And never again
Will we lie

Spoiled Time
Always searching for a light
Nothing seems to be in my life
Well I need some responsibility
There's no one here when I need them to be
Always trying to live by right
Nothing seems to fill my time
All I need is just a picture
Please
Of a place where I could be happy
Crammed it all down inside
Just waiting for the right time
All I needed was a sign
There's no wasting until I'm wasting my time
Is it a waste of my life
To spend my time trying
To help you get away
To stop the crying?
Ignored the facts my friends pointed out to me
The love, the blood, is washed from my eyes and now I see
You played me
Fists clenched tight
And to top it off - my friends were right
Do you want to waste your life
Just awaiting to die?
I don't want to spend my time
Taking part in your lies
The glass of broken thoughts is in my eyes
Is there a way to make things right?
Why do you cry?
Just to prove you're human?
When you need to learn - everything dies
Blacken my eyes
Raging me blind
Just turn away
Give me my time
Time to find

What do you cry for
When there's nothing more?
What time is spoiled
When there's no more time?

Tramp

Yes, I know it's easy
Just like every little thing you do
Yes, I know it's easy
Being spoiled little you
But I bet it can't be too easy
To want everything that you get
I just wish the one I once called mine
Would show a little regret
Yes, I miss you when
I am horny
Yes, I miss you when
I wake up in the morning
But at night
It's you I want to fight
Wish the liar I once called mine
Would get out of my sight
Yes, I think about you when
It's day and night
Yes, I think about you when
I am not right
But sometimes it's you I want to right
Wish the tramp I once called mine
Would just give me time

Loser
Do you know why I have to scream at you?
Understand me
Do you know why I have to hate you?
Answer me
Do you know why I'm better than you?
You're a loser
Such a loser
I don't know why you think you know me
You don't know me
Don't know why you care
Torture me
I know why you suck
You're a loser
Such a loser
Do you know why you are there?
Listen to me
I don't know anyone who cares
Loser
And in my anger
You've made me the winner

Memory Pool
Always day to day
You were just fading away
Whenever I couldn't find what I was trying to say
You were there for me
And no longer can I see you
Nor can I feel you
I need you in my life
A need for a light to be shined
I'm transparent - you can see who I miss
That's why we've all gathered here to reminisce
When I run - I slow down
When I stand - I sink and I drown
Don't want to leave the memories
I often swim backwards in my theories
So I fall
I fall back in the memories
Life is so much colder without you
Love is so worthless without you
I feel helpless without you
My home is empty without you
Sometimes I think there's no time for life to go on
As you walk on
So lonely without you
As I turn my back
It's hard not to react
As you start to pack
I'm so lonesome
Look at me
Lonely ol' me, down again
Swimming in the memories alone
Waiting

Clouding Reality
You know how it is - clouding the sun
Just to block out your confusion
So what's wrong with me?
Is it something I cannot see?
Is it in the air I breathe?
It's so sad
So sad I can't go back
Too bad to go back on my word
And it's down the drain
And you drown in the rain of your world
You know how it is - first come, first serve
On the right track but suddenly you swerve
It's affecting your universal world
The way you learn
Do what you please
Until that certain someone knocks you down
Down to your knees
Everything seems to change
Just a matter of time before it rains
Washes out your world again
I guess life's a little messed up
All kickstarts the pain
When the days get rough
But if it happens again
Do you know how to deal?
Bullets fly and the party starts
When it's all too real
Take a tip from me
What you read and what you see is spaced from what you get
All the shit you believe in - you might as well forget

Revenge
Naked doll hanging from a shoe string
All and all while making love to me
It's my violent fantasy
Come on and soothe me
You're getting me ready
Your words are tripping me
While I was walking steady
Another share of violence
Has taught me well enough
Never to fool with conscience
And when it's had enough
Did you ever stop to think about me?
I bet you lust the feeling
Slipping, undoubtedly into a pool of misery
Life will never be the same
Trust is a forgetful theme
That is a crying shame
Sweet revenge is the name of the game
No one will remember your name
Stardom is but a shiny gleam
That is a crying shame
Sweet revenge is the name of the game
I hear whispers lie
My sweet distance dies
Deceived and left me alone
Autophobic out here on my own
But you don't know
You don't know the truth
Between me and you
How much longer before we breakdown?
Don't let whispers clown
I will let you down
Why do you deny
My sweet reasons why?
Delayed and played
Twisted me so violently

And all along the doll was in my mind
Your trust was all in my mind
But the revenge is sweet
And it is mine

Responsibility

Another day
Another step
Another way my love is kept
A change of heart
Another time
All confused by this messed up rhyme
Another answer
Yet no more questions
All thrown out by crooked propositions
Another soul
Another life
No responsibility is taken in line
Darkness walls
Darkness tides
Flowing jaggedly, young troubled minds
You wear your mask, I'll wear mine
Darkness falls
Darkness hides
Flowing smoothly through violent minds
Hide behind your mask, I'll hide behind mine
Never knew this to be so far
As a martyr, I'm my own tragic scar
Though I can't deny my harbingers
In another time
Another body
She re-arranges the violence
And she separates her conscience
She'll eventually break the silence
Responsibility taken in strides

Poetry in Violence
Fumble my faith
Awaiting my fate
Close behind my wrath
As we follow my path
Into silence
Silence
Poetry in violence
Lighting it up like an arson baby would
Only to become more jagged than beneath the ground I stood
Upon the gold-plated sun
Appeared an image that, when it was done
It spoke to me in ways, I was stunned
Said 'do what you have to do-
To get closer to you'
Inner me
Deeper than the red I bleed
The lyrics I breathe
Irritating our minds like a sinus
We're both deafened by silence
So in the kindness of mayhem
We can't deny the poetry in violence

Trust & Change
Hollow earth, empty world
No freewill in a world where everything changes
And nothing's the same
But you
In this day's age
Where everyone fears change
But you
You kept it true
Without you
Torn in two
Broken into
Can change,
Would change
Could change
Will change, will trust
Would you trust in me
If I trusted you?
Don't owe me anything
I'll never owe you
Another night I spend to think
To dream of you
And everything
We've been through
You've never left me
Always stayed true to me
It's not easy
To say I'm sorry
And it's not easy
So say I love you
To mean it so true
Like I do
And when I hang my
Head to cry
You are there to dry
My teary eyes

Shreds of Pity
I forget my purpose when I drop my head to cry
I can't explain why
Just seems to fall apart right before my eyes
So I look to you for guidance
Just to have someone to look up to
There to break my silence
Someone to call my friend
Someone to run to
I try to look in the mirror
Just to prove myself wrong
Always searching for alternatives
Just so I don't have to try so long
Why do I feel so far away?
I don't think I can last another day
Why do I have to feel this way?
Can't this all just go away?
Some days I just want to drift away
Away from all the pain and despair
Wish I could just disappear
Every time the thought of suicide gets in my mind
My purpose seems bent
The thought of taking my life just to let you vent
I get you heated, make you mad
Kill myself, make you sad
Sad for me
Shreds of pity
Joe after Joe I see
Nobody seems to think like me
Misunderstanding of probability
I've been pulling this load so far
Living life is so hard
Going through all this trouble and pain is a living hell
Makes me wonder what life will be like without me
But why would I do that?
Am I not strong enough?

Lost Friends
It fades to black
And it takes me so far
So far that I can't trace it back
When it comes down, it comes down hard
It comes down stacked
Relationships are hard to come by
But when you find them, you either want to hold too tight or turn your back
I try to run when I can't decide
All I can think is, do I have a place to hide?
Wake up every morning, get out of bed
Take a look at my life and realize it's all in my head
Shallow - like the end we are swimming in
Broken - like my trust in them as friends
Shattered - like my faith within
Skating - on ice so thin
And then I fall off the wall
Left to crawl down the hall
I try to think but I can't find my head
All I really know are the things they said

Gone
I'm staring at my clock again
Same time as it was back then
Nothing will ever make this change
I guess it will remain the same
I'm speaking 'round in circles
Tripping over my words
Nobody knows for certain
But we can expect the worst
Can't believe I'd be infected by you
I guess an end was well over due
So it's time to say goodnight
As I walk on towards the door
That's when I realize
This will be no more
I said "I love you."
You said "I hate you."
Another day without you
And I still miss you
You and your everything
You and your everything burn
I said "I can't believe you."
You said "We're through."
Another day with this stitch
Why so blind? I couldn't see it
Why dwell over you?
You and your everything
You and your everything burn
You're an ulcer
An ulcer
Questions over comfort
It's all a hurt
Now a subject of pity
My life, leave me to lead
You're killing me
You're my cancer core
And I don't want you anymore
But I do thank you for pointing this out
Now that I think of all the times
You treated me like slime

It was a crime to waste my time
Loving you, believing you when it was said
I said "Until death do us part."
When you said "Not even when we're dead"
I never thought my belief would tear us apart
Now my life is lost in the dark
I can't believe you when you say
Maybe I can love again someday
I can't believe it, he had you turned
I can't believe it, you had me burned
I can't take all this at once, I need some relief
It's the lie in believe that gets to me
Some days I wish I had never found you
Some days I wish I could just forget you
Some days I wish we could be through
But nothing really happens the way you want it to
Sometime I will find my state of mind
Sometime I will find my piece of the pie
Sometime I will find that something that gets me by
But when you want it to, time never flies by
Leave me now, down and out
Now that I'm gone, I'm gone
Some days I wish I...
Sometime I will find my...
Now that I'm gone, I'm gone.....

Youth Catching Up
Life was so much better as a kid
If I could only tell you about the things we did
Time is so much different
Since the days that came and went
You want to be young
You say that you're old and done
If you could count the breaths of your lung
With all the stories you've told
Seeming unimportant due to your age
It's you who controls your life
It's you who seizes the day
Let's stay
Stay young
Life is short, time flies by
Home flashes right before my eyes
I'm told this will never last forever
All these feelings I have for you
Will they still be here tomorrow?
Will you be by my side?
Am I sleeping by myself tonight?
Questions I thought I'd ask
Answers coming back to bite me in the ass
Have you thought all this through?
I'm waiting here for you
What else do you need?
I need to know now
Will this ever last?
Or will it all come back and bite me in the ass?

Empty Tanks and Empty Shoes
Just another pain
The pain in my face
Get the hell out
You know the way
Just another day
A day where I have to fake all this again
Why does it take a lie to pull you from my skin?
This situation will never blow over
You've said your peace
Now I'll say mine
Found more hate than I thought I could ever find
Locked our love away with vows like a treasure to never find again
Your joke is killing me
So much for loving need
Do it again so I can see
The way you did me
You know my tank is running on empty
I don't have any faith left for you
I know you always say you love me
But I know that can't be true
I saw you staring at them
Thinking they can love you more than I
So you decide to run with them
I guess I'll go lie down and die
I think you should stop
I think you have the time
I also think you should take it and realize what all you have in life and why
Be true to you before you find yourself sinking into someone else's shoes

Nothing
Don't you ever wish
What you dreamt was true?
Don't you ever wish
It was all for you?
Don't you ever wish
The sun would come
And send all the clouds
To run?
Don't you ever wish
Your life away
Because you never know
This could be your day
And so you find me here
Wrapped up in salty tears
That have grown
All through the years
Another day without you here
Makes thoughts seem so unclear
Unsure with all that I hear
I just need to know you're near
A need to know what's gotten me by all these years
Another day of passing time
So short yet so long in line
I can't find myself to do what I want to
Crawled up into your mind
Looking for a reason to find
Behind, we'll know a significance of some kind
There is nowhere to run
When there is no one to hide from
Get over it –
You're running from nothing

A High School Romance (Though One-Sided)
There she is
She's so pretty
What is this?
I have a strong, strong feeling
Whenever I talk to her
I forget what to say, can I buy a vowel?
Whenever I look at her
My knees buckle up and I fall down
I hope she's here today
But what do I say?
Do I ask her out now or wait a day?
"Whenever I'm near you
Do you get these feelings too?
It's a nice day outside
Can I borrow your study guide?
Want to go out tonight?"
Just another thoughtful day
I can't see the sunshine
Through the fields of gray
I can't help wondering what she's doing today
Probably just a lonely night
I can't see the stars
Through the sea of bright
I can't help wondering what she's doing tonight

Chump
I won't sit here
Tell you how much life sucks
And I won't tell you how
Your time is up or how you've had enough
I'm sure you've figured it out by now
The holes you've punched in me
Aren't a sting as they used to be
And I'm not bitter
This isn't about 'O woe is me'
It's about the in-betweens
And all the holes we leave
Hey, what do I mean to you?
What do you mean to me?
Empty
Just look inside of me
The best thing
That's ever happened to me
Turned out to be
My worst enemy
And how do you think I feel?
Like a chump
And if she gave me a second chance
I'm sure I'd have to pass
Because I'm not *that* much of a chump
Tired
Of the same old thing
It's not you
But it sure isn't me
A dark storm
Deep in me
Everything torn
Everything
I was the greatest thing she'll ever pass
She'll never get a second chance
Now tell me
Who's the chump?

Daddy Dear
Brand new rich kids giving to the poor
What are you looking for?
Never helping, selfish needs only wanting more
What are you looking for?
Filthy rich and rotten to the core
Daddy's little girl searching for a man
What are you looking for?
Said she wanted something to fit perfect on her hand
What are you looking for?
No one to help since she stole from daddy dear
What are you looking for?
Drowning in her financial quicksand

Expired

No matter how hard I try
I just can't deny
That you trust a lot more than those who pose as perfectly fine
Squirm around on the floor
Like a dog without a spine
I promised I'd take it to my grave
Loved and admired as brave
And it's just thinking about us
That drives these insane notions and visions
In my brain
Why do I ask myself questions
That I know I can't answer?
You can only just imagine
All the pain
Why do you ask me so-so questions
When I know what you're after?
Come out and tell me
Please just say
I'm sick - I'm tired
I can't take this
My brain is expired

The Thin Line between Anger & Remorse
It's not easy to hide
I'm angry
Don't know why
Stuffed it all down
Year after year
Try to ignore it all
It just gets worse from here
So you're in arm's reach
You're all around me
I can see that clearly
It's been so long since this has been home
I'm alone in this hole
I don't blame you
I don't blame me
I just want to know why it's happening
All this anger
All this pain
Can't let it take the best of me
I can point and I can blame
Doesn't matter now, it won't change a thing
I think we've come a long way
Not a day goes by
That I don't think about throwing this all away
Don't worry about a thing
I'll take all the blame with me
Please don't drop everything
Just to run away with me
Don't worry
I'll take all the memory
When I take my leave
I'm sorry for everything I've done
So sorry to take this all and run
I'm sorry for any pain I've brought
So sorry for anyone I've lost

Pause the World
I know
I've wasted time with her
Tonight
I'm here to say I'm all for you
You know
I'd throw myself at you
Tonight
I'm here and I'm here to do just that
Do you think things will ever be the same?
Same as it ever was?
Chocolate?
A dozen roses?
"I'm sorry, dear. Please come back to me."?
When I hold your hand
I feel so changed - a new man
Time is changing
Can't help but to wonder why you don't accept
Life is re-arranging
Through the pain, changing of the seasons is all I have left
Can you spare a dime?
Night's young, there's still time
I have to make a call
I've just got a lot on my mind
Can we stop time to reflect on life?
Can we stop this tonight?
Why fight change?
Is it tearing us apart?
Time changes, it's what you have left in your heart
Why can't you see?
I see
Why can't we pause the world tonight?
It just feels right

Death Quilt
Want to see a fight?
Look to the stars tonight
Who will come together?
Who will make it right?
Making things right with a style of light
More NASA research
Making everything tight with the universe
To deny the pain's surprise
To pass up the soulful cries
And to despise the dreadful sighs
There's a secret satellite
And it's taking over tonight
Poisonous conscience
Snake bite, spider bitten
This old woman knittin'
A quilt of death
To say the rest
Rest in peace
On a spiritual leash
Say goodnight and realize
Everything you once despised
Is sucked in your life by black hole eyes

Anti-Ballad
You molded me
Now around you I can't be me
I just wanted to be friends
But you needed things your way
You had to change me
I can never be myself
When I'm with you
Because I'm already someone else
You chose to end me
Chose to make me into something
I just wanted to chill with you
And have you like me for myself
But instead you made me something new
No one needed to change me
If I'm going to at all
Let me change on my own
I can never be myself
When I'm with you
Because I'm already someone else
Just in the way you talk to me
I can't believe anymore
The way you change me so easily
I can't believe you
The way you act towards me
I can't believe this is you
The way you quit me so easily
I can't believe that we're through
Can't believe I fell in love with such a piece of shit
Embarrassed, so I won't admit it
You want to take this for granted
Well here's your anti-ballad
There's no more time
It was all for you
And when you left
My time went too

Stay With Me

Please stay
Don't leave me right away
Just let me know you
I want to
Need to
Know the truth
Stay
Don't leave me alone
I want you to stay
Don't go away
Away
Don't leave me home
All alone
Alone
I want you to see me in twenty
See what I've become
The lonely
Stay
Don't leave me alone
Don't leave me today
Not today
No, not today

My Condition
You don't listen to me at all
You don't care about my problems
You don't care at all
Because what I say
Is that you don't give a damn
Because if I pay
You back it's because I can
So I was spitting on your flame so lit
When you were talking shit
I always knew you were careless
I don't want to carry you anymore
I don't want to deal with your poorness
Poorness at heart
And your lack of wisdom
Tore us apart
I can see through you like the window you are
I can see just how you are
Fragile and clear, can see through so far
I can see
Go ahead and stab me in the back
It's just a feeling, a feeling I had for you
I feel this, too
Lack of faith leaves us all alone
Departure is what takes us from our homes
As I lie here in bed watching thoughts run rapid in my head
Something in mind occurs
The sensation I feel just burns
I can't see my face
I guess it's fallen back in its place
Between our love and our insults - that little space
I wish that I could speak to you
One last time before I'm through
Leave this be and say goodbye to you
Now that your life is a mess and gone to hell
You're looking for someone to blame, well
Blame yourself
When I sit by that window
I wonder, 'where did you go?'
Catch a cold draft bringing you back in memory

That came and left me hanging
I was hanging on the ledge
Little did you know how close I was to the edge
If I could see you one more time I'd get a glance
Also, went the tendencies to kill you when I had a chance
What happened with our friction?
Take a picture because now's the only time you get to see nonfiction
But it's fictitious; it's all been a sham
With all the hate thrown around
But you don't care how empty I am
On the inside, tears to my eyes so sad
You'll never realize what we had
Box of our prize possessions
Threw it out
I've grown out of my condition
You tried to pull me down
Tried to pull me away
But you can't tear me down
Now that I'm wide awake

Fire and Grind
So crippled - can't believe
Nobody to adore
So lost - can't retrieve
Nobody to ignore
So twisted and I don't care
Nobody to give a damn
Is anybody there?
Hear me if you can
I've lost all of me
Forget today so easily
Are you not satisfied?
He grew up to be more man than I
Oh, aren't you satisfied
Realizing he can survive beyond this tide
So about tomorrow, forget the next day
I didn't want to be here anyway
So forget about tomorrow if it's not too late
I don't need any more in my way
Can't you see the line?
We cross to get to where we are
You know I could have lied
But we've been through this before
Okay
I can't wait for tomorrow, and then the next day
So I can see that look on your face

Circles Around Dreams
I can't call life a circle
Because I'm never back home
Will power's not too strong
And I've been running away for too long
Sitting here in this cold seat
Alone yet everyone's around me
So crowded no one can see
And everyone has their own story
Do you ever wonder what's behind the fame?
Underneath it all, a mask of wealth, is pain
Glory days come and go but always seem the same
If we could only know the loneliness in fame
Money deceives your mind of reality
But it's all building up to one fine memory
I want to be like you
I want to be somebody, too
Here comes the age old song
The tune life plays for me
Watch out, the age old song
Listen for that tune God chose for me
As fast as wheels turn
Listening for that tune
Paranoia really burns
And my stomach turns
And I misunderstand
I'm back where I started
Right where I began
And it remains the same

Dead to the World
Yes I'm hearing what you're saying
I don't know why
I don't need your lie
I don't need or want to be under your authority
All it is, this power, straight to your head
To your world I might as well be dead
Time to mute the world
Not another word
Your voice slurs
Dead to the world
Never listened to a word I said
Might as well be dead
Dead to the world
I'm not sleeping
Yet I'm dreaming
They all point and stare
They'd be bored knowing I don't care
Daydreaming in class
Awaiting time to pass
They all wonder what's in my head
Nothing in subject
All thoughts are dead
Dreaming in day
No attention to pay
Dead to the world

A Curious Nature
I take you out
Bring you home
Shut them out
And we're alone
I select you
I direct you
Inspecting your reason
I dissect you
Your melting begins
Coats over like a second skin
But your screams
They blend to mend over the seams
I cut away what's left of your picture
And I fight what's left of this night
And its curious nature

Image of Suffering
Your silence is what kills me
Makes me feel so damn ugly
Because you won't talk
Never express your feelings
You just walk all this off once again
Lock me up inside my room
I'll wait for you sitting in the gloom
Could never tell anything to you
You would shut me up when I began
You just walk all this off once again
You're coding in your silence
I can't see through this
I can only hear the sirens
You and all your violence
Set from sense
Brought this on by your lack of self esteem
No more sun
It's all just a gleam
That light from the whites of your eyes blinding me
Drop your image of suffering
Drop it
Drop your image of suffering

Letters & Ladders

Reading your letter over and over a dozen times
Sparking the raging emotions of a thousand mimes
Hormones are driving me too
I want you to love me
But I won't force you to
Two days on this letter
You'd think I'd be through, but no
Everything is getting better
That's why I can't chance
Letting you go
You're my missing link
But I fear I might lose you if I blink
Ran away for a reason
Now getting back to you is my mission
Weeks upon this ladder of golden bars
I could either step down to you
Or climb up to the stars

Want and Need
Something for you to hear
Nothing for them to say
Would you like a ticket out of here?
Or would you like to stay?
Anything to help you from feeling this way
They only care about their money
They never have time for you
A call to open arms
I don't blame you
So what if you can't do all the things that you want to
Anything you can do
Take pride because you can
Be proud of what you can get away with
What the world wants
And what the world needs
Isn't exactly the way I see things
Do what you want to
There's nothing holding you back but you
Anything I can do?
Yes, I take pride in helping you
Be proud of what you can get away with
Because what the world wants
And what the world needs
Isn't exactly the way I see things

Remorse

Where was I?
When you needed someone to hear your side
Where was I?
When it was cold out and no one would let you inside
Where was I?
When you needed someone to talk to
Where was I?
When I heard this is what you were going to do
Where was I?
When you were pulling the trigger just to end it all
Where was I?
When all the other times I'd catch you when you'd fall
It's too late now - all I can say
I'm sorry things just change
You just needed someone to rely on
Where was I?

Hatchets
I remember the days of old and new
I remember the times with you
I once was in love with you
But now I guess that's through
Every day's a new tomorrow
That we will not live in sorrow
Let's bury the hatchet
Just in case we haven't

Christmas For A Dear Friend
To lose your everything
Every day and every way
Needing just a little something something
Broke with nothing to say
You'll find your way
Don't worry
It's just a matter of time
And time is all you really have
Wish there was something beneath the tree
Maybe an envelope with your name
A little something from me

My Sweet Fire
All but she remembers
Why I tried so hard for her
She doesn't realize her importance
My everything
She's a sweet fire
Burning passionate lover
She burns
Emitting embers and cinders
So I can see her
My sweet fire

Nevermore
Never
Couldn't want more for you
Never
Could not want much more for you
Nevermore
Never
Couldn't hope for more than this
Never
Could not expect much more from this
Nevermore

Here
Does your conscience tend to weigh you down?
Do you talk about life when no one's around?
Soliloquies, they pave the way for your insanity
Can you please tell me why you throw away responsibility?
Does your conscience make it hard to unwind?
Do your reasons cloud your mind?
Your actions, they pave the way for your destiny
But can you please tell me why you avoid reality?
Why do you plague yourself with dreaming?
Can't you get a grip on reality?
Get a hold of what's really real?
Just take your time
And understand
I will always be here to lend a hand

Brass Ring
Let it all out
Anti-social, trapped in a shell
So I need to break out
Leave me alone
I want to top my day off with a nice come home
I want to visit a land of no return
It sure beats getting burnt
I guess I just haven't learned to deal
To deal with what is real
Respect for what is lost
Has been found but for a cost
Can respect be written around?
What's been going down?
Can I leave it where it's been?
I just end up finding it again
But only within myself

Excuses Excuses
Sometimes I see my problems
I often think of ways to solve them
Sometimes I seem so careless
That's when light fades to darkness
Sometimes I think too much - I can't choose
Every time I think I'll win - I lose
Sometimes I feel so helpless
But there's no excuses

Motivation Wanted
Your touch
My crush
Love causes thrush
It's a far stretch
I bet
I can forgive but I still regret
Always giving up
Nothing motivates
Nothing shields from the hate
No more clean slates
Nothing shields from fate
Never been one to speak out
Or been one to rush
But sometimes I just want something behind me to push

Fly Paper
Stereotype me
Living proof of identity crisis
Reality is stretching far from your fantasy
It's your choice; I'll leave it up to you
You think you're stuck
Well I'm stuck too
In a forbidden race
A case of false identity
Truth is far from your face
You disrespect me, I disrespect you
You think you're stuck?
Well I'm stuck too
Have I been left behind?
Good thoughts would be nice
Grab my mind, shake it like dice
The world doesn't revolve around you
You think you're stuck?
Well I'm stuck too
Caught up
Flypaper
Stuck
Can't move

Forgiveness
I tried
To please you
Like I usually do
I lied
To you
Doesn't matter now, I always do
I don't want your way
I don't need your faith
Leave me here, I lie awake
So I lie here in bed
Watching thoughts run loose in my head
Time to think is all I had
Why did I choose to make you mad
I'm sorry
I don't know what I was thinking
All I needed to do was say something
Please forgive me

Top Boss Bonus Level
Fate, destiny, plenty of miles away
Faith, loving need, kept from me, mind's slipping away
The best
The rest
How could I pass the test?
If there were something to show
Nobody knows which way the wind blows
It's all in the way you hold your own
Another bark, another moan
Throw this dog a bone
Something to throw
Somewhere to go
But a need to bleed to prove I'm real
The reality of the matter gets to flow
I feel I can fight another day
Been through too much to walk away
It's such a long way from here so I'll stay
The lessons
Everything I've learned
The essentials
The nothings I've earned
Erased competition to get where I am today
So I'll stay

Our Time
Your pleasure becomes my pain
Your sunshine becomes my rain
Your puddle of tears becomes my ocean
Your thoughts, your fears become my emotion
Your dream becomes my nightmare
Your part becomes my share
Your winter becomes my springtime
Your actions become my rhyme
Use emotion as your fuel
Save your wits, keep them for the duel
Save the time
Our time

6 Sides To A Prison
Chop me up
Condemn me in my pieces
I've had enough
Condemn me in my grievances
I'm through with all the voices in my mind
The haunting silence and glitches in time
Lock me up
In this box
I'm fed up
Nothing but bloody smocks
I've had a lot of shadows in my past
Lost them all
Youth moves too fast
I feel I'm trapped in a box
The nothings around me are closing in tightly
Surrounded by locks
I believe something you say may brighten my day
But probably not
This six-sided prison encloses me
Inside, inside, inside
If I move too fast will I break like glass?
I feel so fragile
Break me now
Break me down
Break me out
It's time to break out
No more boxes
Not even bricks
Just thick slabs of emptiness
And all I count is six

Cold Distance
Why is it that you walk away?
Is it something I said or need to say?
Maybe I should apologize
Make things the way they used to be
Now every time I take a look
You seem more distant to me
So close yet still far away
I need to know what left you this way
And although you said you'd never change
You came back different when you had left the same

Secondary Hearts
So when did I become secondary
Back of the line in your priority
Thought you could play me
Often thought I was a puppet
No doubt I'm gullible
Surface of truth - no way to touch it
Can't catch grasp on reality
Put my whole world on hold, just waiting for you to go
But when you did not leave, I figured it was a good sign
No sight of playing
Involved in everything - no lie, I was your game
I bet if you ask her today, she doesn't even remember my name
Can't catch grasp on reality
Where did yesterday go?
Down the drain
Why did I waste my time
Taking part in your game
When will be tomorrow
I need another day
Can't believe I threw off my life
Just for you to stay

Blame
It killed my pride
Trying to keep you inside
Such a long ride
Now that you've brought it all on...
It hurt my eyes
Trying to see through your ways
I've sewn them shut so the tears will never cry
Yet they never dry
Now that you've brought it all on...
I know you feel this too
And I don't blame me
I blame you

Don't Tell Me
Don't tell me to breathe in
Everything you say just sinks in
No time for change
It all seems the same
So walk your paths
Walk until you end up back
Now that you're home - step back
Don't tell me to breathe in
Everything I see just closes in
No time to re-arrange
The promises you made don't mean a thing
How many times can you tell a lie?
Is it once in a while or once in a lifetime?
Don't tell me to breathe in
I suffocate myself for a reason
Don't tell me about my pride
I'll decide what this is inside
I can't hide or attempt to try
To shield myself from this night
Look into my eyes
All your silence - never golden
And my mind keeps on unfolding
Never knowing which way to go
If there was an answer I should know
Please tell me before I go
Don't tell me
Anything but what I need

Toxic Addict
You've got this clouding lie
Only half of what you deny
You've got the sweetness
To cover up your poisons
You've got the cancer
Becoming death's dancer
With you drowning in quicksand
Could I lend you a hand?
Give it a little while; you'll believe your own lie
Time to unfold into truth, I don't know why
But you'll think it's right
Played by the mind's eye
Hold the truth captive until you die
Pathological
The logical yet less educational
This toxic fib addict
Is drama magnetic

Under Your Rain
The years fly by
Faster than I can stand
I don't understand why I cry
Despite it being wrong, I'd figure again
When you're near, I see rain
Can't let these days go by
I never tried to understand
I just laid back down and cried
I'd run away if I could stand
Time is a grip and it won't let go
How could you know?
Words cannot flow
But enough to say I'd like to see you again
When you're here, I see rain

Time To Cry

Life's a little strange
The way it decides to change
Could fight the media for a purpose
A matter of time before it starts to surface
But now you want to deny
What's keeping you alive
Let it all come out when it's time to cry
Brought to my attention again
What's up with pain
That hate tends to claim?
And why are you the one to blame
When the dark cloud begins to rain?
Let it all come out when it's time to cry

A Fool for You
I cannot fight the feeling
How long before I find the meaning
Never seems to change the reading
Surprisingly so misleading
Just want to know the real you
The truth
I'm in this maze for you
I'll never find the meaning
Never fight the feeling
Never change the readings
Still misleading
Just wish I had a clue
I'm in this maze for you
It's nothing about how you don't understand
Drawing a blank - nothing to me right off hand
How can I tell someone I don't know
What they went through?
How can I tell you
Just let you know
My feelings are true
But let me tell you
I'm a fool
For falling in love
I'm a fool
For all I've done
And I'm a fool
A fool for you

Pointless
Told you once and I'll tell you again
All I wanted was to be friends
Just a little something harmless
Yet everything is pointless
First a start and then it ends
One slip - a backwards bend
One good deed to feed the homeless
Yet everything's pointless
Glass - our only divide
Aging with every stride
Nothing seems to relieve stress
Yet everything's pointless
I can never promise truth but I'll tell you no lies
All I see is the world through my eyes
So on short notice stress
What exactly is pointless?

Destiny
Walking around
Town to town
Trying to find my way
All that is found
Is dreams shot down
And I don't know how long
I can stay on
Before being shoved off
Pushed away
Open my eyes to see my way
Alone at night
In my bed dreaming
It's not going to happen
If I'm just believing
Had a little
Had a lot
And now I'm left behind
Could you give me a taste of what it's like to be blind?
There are plenty of stars in the sky for me
All I have to do is stand up and reach

Counterfeit Death (And Dodging the Debt)
Death unto death
Now that I think about life I don't want to pay my debt
Don't want to pay your debt
Death unto death
With an all new lineup
Choices dying for a pick up
Cut yourself to bleed
Never feel the need
Counterfeit debt
From life throughout death
Counterfeit death
Faking light sight for a life debt

Sweet Little Death
All clouds are lifting
So I can see
All clouds are lifting
So I'll be free
Next time I'll choose someone else's death to fool with
Next time I'll find a sweet little death that doesn't want me
When will this sweet little death be through with me?
No next time for me
This sweet little death has its grip on me
They all follow and they're following
They all follow and they're following me
All clouds have lifted
So now I see
All clouds have lifted
And now I'm free

In The Cards
You give up a lot
You take what you give
You ruin life's plot
So in return you'll live
You take what you will
You breathe what you kill
You get what you put in
It's reality sinking in
The world's an imperfect place
Always cracks in the face
Of time and time again
And you think I hate you
For making the world so bad
And depressing that I have to write this all down
To get it off my chest
And my stomach still turns out the size of the ulcers
You placed in my heart
Yes, I think you're heartless
But I guess it's what is willed for me
And it is willed to be
So shall it be written
So shall it be done

Some Kind of Hero
So you want to save the world
When you're just helping yourself
You're not in it for the happy ending but the glory
The money
There's no shovel to get yourself out of this hole
You want to save yourself from this hell
But society knows you can only save who you care for
You only care for yourself
You are no superhero
You think you are going to protect
While if you reflect, you'll find more than you would ever detect
You're not our savior
You'll never get over your behavior
Money doesn't make you the hero
But did you know?
I don't think so
You are no superhero
Another false role model commercialized today
Just put out in the world to see if they can change their ways
You are no superhero

Clean

I love you
I hate you
I'm so confused
I love you
I hate you
What am I to do
Is there some way-
Out of this mess I've made?
I can't fly so high anymore
I just don't know what to do anymore
I love you
I hate you
Can't go on without you
I love you
I hate you
Oh what to do
Is there some way-
Out of this mess I've made?
This is a land slide
Why do you wash me away so?
Let me go
Why?
Why do you let me go?
I'm your filth
You're my soap
And you wash me away so

The Inner Enemy
Failure gripping your stomach
Hearing your heartbeat fall short a few
Fingertips numbing
Numbing
You can't feel your face long enough to peel it off
A wicked strain in your veins
Pulling away
Denying the memory
You were who you were
You are who you are
No more turning away
You must face yourself
Before it's too late

Dead Last

Laced it, went on and faced it
Disgraced, can't show your face
Lost the race and fell from grace
Failed to make contact with base
When you need to reach out and touch faith
It's never within your grasp
You'll never grab what you can't have
Took a bite on your behalf
Felt the wrath of the aftermath
Been slacking - dead last
Swallowed by the shadows in your past
Shoulder devil gets the last laugh
Broke records in half to test yourself to see how far you'd last
That's right, always reaching for something you can never grab
Always wanting something you can never have
Always missing the reality you are forced to grasp
Now that you need me back
You can't have me, though you want it so bad
Somebody's got to know why
The further I'm pulled away
The more I want to see your face
Just like a phone, forbidden fruit can go both ways
As it's you I cannot reach
You will never get me
No matter how bad I want it to be

Ego Waves
Look at you
All ego
What happened to you?
Where did you go?
Empty boulder
The big head on your shoulders
I saw this in a dream
But in the end
You're not my friend
Hey big shot
Made your way out of small time
Give me your best shot
But remember you're from the same small town and same hard times
Your waters are getting too high for you to breathe
And you can't swim
Drown, drown, drown
In ego waves
Didn't you ever find the way out?
You say no but I think you did
You stepped out and then back in
I think you enjoy the game
All you really wanted was the fame
Despite the stretches of the pain
Will you ever find the way out?
Out of ego waves?

Anthems in the Shade
Now here's a quick anthem for your brain
Buckshot rhymes spread even through thick rain
Make the right choice within your head
Walk the right path or you'll end up dead
Drugs? You should be selling words instead
You must believe in these words I've said
Don't get carried away
The sway of the ricochet
Awaiting the sundown everyday
In my face every day
The pain is pointed out to me again
All alone, I can't shake this
Depression's a must
Stereotyping teen rebelliousness
Is this hell?
No one to talk to but myself
Lost souls
In the valleys with tossed olds
I watch as you shed your skin
Your broken in-
Shells
Aftermath of the white lies you tell
It's all like the glass you smash
Attacking your spine like whiplash
Like the mirror your look into
A spell you can't undo
You're broken too
In my mind
In the flesh
Comes a time
The caress
Will remind me
When to rest
Want to make my day?
Whose day's made?
Turn away
Just keep it all in shade

Life Imitating Art
I'm sorry to do this
But I can't do this anymore
Yes, there's someone else
But it's someone else I adore
From the bottom of my heart
I thank you for always being there
In my time of need
My apologies for wasting yours

Realization
Decaying life receipt
What a relief
Finally understanding my needs
Look in the mirror
Look real hard
Reflections at various speeds
If I gain all today
That's because all I have to gain
Is everything
What are the odds I lose it all again?
If it's gone tomorrow I'll never know what might have been
No reason to fake my pain
It'll all come back again
I am who I am, I feel what I feel
Still scared and helpless - I fear what I fear
I just need to vent

Dream Streaming
Life will drag you out
Life will drop you down
Life will punk you out
Life will run you down
Why is it now that we decide to be run down?
Life is tough, now you know
Trying is rough, but don't let go
Don't let go of your dreams and you'll succeed
Don't hold back - let it all out and scream
Don't hide your pain, let it flow through your stream
Drink from the stream
Bird's eye view of a dream
Counts the shooting stars
Wishes you knew how important you are
For someone to lean upon
No one too strong
A need essential to say the least
All you'll need is help to slay the beast
Don't waste your life
You don't have forever
All the time in the world
Is only down on paper
If you let it eat you
Spit you back out
Your morals are see-through
Pour yourself back up the spout

Self Portrait
Fall into the haze
Gaze at the maze
Fall into the haze of your self portrait
Stumble inside and walk through a maze that's needed
Try not to fall in life so hard if you can help it
All I have to say
You can't take away
Forget it - it's *your* self portrait
You brought this on yourself
So when you complain about living in hell
Look in the mirror, see what you've turned into
Because I'm through
It really hurts to say all this
Fall in the haze and gaze at your self portrait

Within
Within is where I know
I could never be alone
Dropping to the bottom I find
That some lights just never shine
Life is a dark place that holds you within
What are the odds we find ourselves again?
Sometimes I feel like I've just let go
Is it okay now? I just don't know
Have you ever ran behind the wind?
Walk alone and let your soul pull you within
Emotions fade, my mind can't flow
When I'm here, every time, you're in my shadow
Within is all I know
Every time you're in my shadow
As I drop to the bottom I find
Some lights just never shine
All alone I sit and I cry
Alone, I'll probably die
And somewhere in between
I'd like to join the scheme
Become part of life
But all is strife
Too much, I ask why
With all this, I can't solve
So why
Within, my problems just evolve
Can't blame anyone else
For why I'm sitting on the shelf
Get into my life
And spend my time within
Why can't this be somebody else?
Why can't this be you?

Vomit Tattoo
I can't tell you what you mean to me
You mean so much to me
That I can't stand
To hear you crying
I cannot stand to be around you
I have bitten my tongue blue
You don't know what you put me through
I've washed my hands of you and you and you and you
I can't tell you what you mean to me
You rage me blind so that I cannot see
With all the wool you've pulled over my eyes
I can't stand to...
I have bitten...
You don't know what...
I've washed my hands of...
Just want to puke with all your asking why
Deceived by lies
Deceiving eyes
The eyes are watching you die
They are all ignoring your cries
Do you envy the clown that never frowns?
Even when no one's around?
Claw into the cave walls
Searching for the answer never found at all
Sadness - lost doll
Broken when fallen
Puke out all your inhuman cries
Puke out your vomit tattoo of the world
Until you are through

Feeding Darkness Still
Drowning
In my own tide
Homicide
Genocide
All the same
Suicide
Though you're alive you're dead inside
Empty
I promise not to hide
And if the truth sets me free
I promise no more lies
Feeding darkness still
Fed to shadows I feel
Denying what is real
The sadness clouds over me
Locked away, pride's so ugly
Danger sleeping next to me
Brain blinded so narrowly
The end is nearing
So help me
Motivate me
Oh sadness - please leave me

Machines on the Edge of Heartache
Cut me some slack
And just step back
I don't want your face
I need my space
Not here
Can you hear?
Disappear
Stop slipping on your tears
So dry that up before you start to rust
Let it all turn into dust
And roll in the wind
When it all goes to bust
I'm not coming around again

To Be Held (and Withheld)
It's raining
But only in here
It's raining
But only your tears
Well if I could keep all the pain from coming in
I'd be your personal medicine
If I could take away the rain
I'd be your personal drain
You walk away
But you walk away from me
You walk away
But you walk away crying
Well If I could block it all
I'd be your personal wall
And if I could carry the mass
I'd be your personal glass
Just one day
One day
For just the two of us
Forget the world around us
In my heart
You play your part
And it's where I want to be
In your arms

Goodbye, My Dear

You say you can't take this
And you're moving away
There's no time to practice
Begging you to stay
I know this life comes underhand
But if you choose to leave it all
I'll never see you again
I know with this life comes an undertow
And this letter shouldn't stop you from go
Going
Gone
I know this night was a bit much
All I can do to heal your cuts
Medicine's never fit in
Emotion's always held strongly within
Your heart
Just came by to say goodnight
I know it's been a long day
I want to tell you goodbye
Just don't know how to say
Just don't know what to say
I guess 'so long, goodnight'
I know this is right
Goodnight to your life
So long
Goodbye, my dear
Live well

Rewire the Waking Mechanism
My head's empty
A glass sphere that sits upon my shoulders
Leaking information into the transparent blue sky
Thoughts flying every which way
Like a mental highway
Waiting for that brutal wreck
Which seems to end lives too quickly
Anxious
Scrawl in the tide
Dig in the sky
Crawl away to hide
Rip out new eyes
I feel the same as I did yesterday
I feel strange
Awake now so wired
Lost in the jungles of liars
Strange feeling getting higher
Cost me desire, my desire
I feel the same as I did yesterday
I feel strange

Who Killed the Saints?

The world is my canvas and I will paint
This world so scandalous
With the crying rain
For pain's sake
This pain's fake
The more I think about this long ride
The longer I will be forced to hide
The world is my canvas and I will paint
The ones who made us feel restraint
For great pain
This paint is rain
And all that's ever gained
Is gained from fallen saints
The world is my canvas and I will paint
The ones who brought us this
And the ones who killed the saints

The Last Laugh
Put a lid on your holiday
Why do you celebrate?
Put out your fire another way
Spent a long time down
With no one around
You held back in your town
At a time you just waited to stuff it all down again
And you want to bring me down with you
Throw yourself to the ground
Act like there's something new
Cry out like a full cloud
Because you know it all revolves around you
Reach your arms out to someone
Nobody's there anyway
Close your eyes - block out sun
No sunlight here - you've shoved it all away
Scream and yell in my face
Spit and cry in disgrace
Feel my pain, lick my soul
Give me more bullshit to fill this hole
So you think you're a hot one?
Well now it's my turn, soon you'll be done
And when I'm finished cutting you down like a tree
I'll have the last laugh - the way it should be

Aftermath

Take away from pain
Run against the grain
We'll all drown in the great rain
I know it sounds insane
I know when I can't stand
And I know when I can't swim
Drop your bomb
Mow the message in your lawn
Stay or crawl away to fight another day
Don't let them push you down
Help the weak up from the ground
Stand up to the powers that be
As strong as you can be
I know there's a time to spar
And I know when I've gone too far
And now I drop the bomb
Now I drop the bomb
And in its aftermath comes hindsight
I watched the dust rise for so long
Now it's all gone
And I've wasted life watching it fall
I thank God I'm alive
As I roll over and die
I tilt my head to the sky
Through the rain in my eye
I see the sunshine
I slip in and out of consciousness
As I wait in line,
A member of the debris

The Difference
Walking down this road again
Passing by where I began
Seemed so right, it seemed so wrong
And that is why this road's so long
And I feel...
And I see...
The difference
You've made in me
Worn down the gravel is
Representing the way we live
I see the faces behind the glass
See the flowers grow as we pass
And I feel...
And I see...
The difference
You've made in me

Brother
Brother, why have you left me here?
Where did you go? Where have you gone?
Brother, why did you leave me here all alone?

Mental Trip
I got a lesson to learn
And plenty of gas to burn
I'm gone
Don't wait up for me
I won't be back until early
Maybe dawn

Pillow
Try to sleep
Cry to sleep
With that big velvet pillow
I gave you last week
Try to sleep
Cry to sleep
With those eyes shut tightly
Thinking about me

Giving Up
Hey, don't be so sad
Hey, it's not that bad
Hey man, you're not cursed
Hey man, it could be worse
Who? Who told you...
Giving up is easier than pushing through?
Hey, don't be thrown
It might be hell but it ain't home
Hey man, you are who you are
It might be out there, but it ain't far
Who? Who told you...
Giving up is easier than pushing through?
Who?

Fallen But Not For Long
We've been through this before
Crying on the floor
Tragedy's at the door
Comedy's right around the corner
Fallen, we've fallen to be weak
Fallen, but we'll back to our feet
We've been through this before
Tragedy's struck some more
Things look bleak today
But hope will swing this way
Fallen, we've fallen to be weak
Though we've fallen
We'll get back to our feet

A Beautiful Mystery
I see her every week
If only there was a name to match the smile
Until then she's nameless
The unknown jewel in which I do not speak of
Pen to paper
They will understand my gorgeous discovery
However I can't touch or taste it
If only I could brush by her once
Instead I stand in a circle of jokers
Exchanging laughs when I'd rather exchange a kiss with her
Her unknown lips
Uncharted territory I long to be in the presence of
And next week will be the same

Smells of Spring
Her hair curls
Curls around my finger
A breath released
A sigh of happiness
Comfortable
Sitting in front of her own home
A lukewarm breeze blows words from my mouth to her ears
And the air she takes in on this day
Breathing in smells of spring

Off to War
I'm going off to war
Probably won't see me no more
I don't believe the cause
When we don't know what we're fighting for
What are we fighting for?
Now I've said my piece
For now my voice remains a memory
I'm going off to war
Probably won't see me no more
Tell mom I love her
I hope she gets this letter
Tell my love I'm sorry
But it's my call to duty
You won't see me no more
Because I'm going off to war

Love & Faith
This is for the reasons at hand
For the men fighting for their land
This is for you and me
For the hands that feed
Sometimes we'll find ourselves in hell
But we'll get out well
All we really need
Is a little love & faith in ourselves
This is for our brothers and sisters
For the tears and blisters
This is for the fathers and mothers
For the love and the lovers
Sometimes we'll find ourselves in hell
But we'll get out well
All we really need
Is a little love & faith in ourselves

No One Sees
Love me
Hate me
Fake me
Put me away
No one sees me
No one sees
Cut me
Burn me
Kill me
Keep me away
No one sees me
No one sees

Corporate Frogs
You may be asking yourself,
"How many of my friends really know me?"
How many of you out there even listen?
Do I even know me?
Do I need to listen?
Corporate frogs, they love to tag me
They'll tag you too; it's just what they do
Name tags and lily pads
But what are we to do?

Out of Water
Please don't fear me
Please don't swim away
Your surface shines
Reflecting light of day
I can't get a hold of you
You slip through my grasp
You're floating through
And it's me you pass
Hey, I'm just like you
I'm just out of water
And my gills are drying out
Drying out singing this to you

Not Knowing
Could it have been there all along?
Will it be there when I'm gone?
I guess I'll never know
And that's just wrong

Parted

It's like an emotional terminator
No one knows where it started
It's like a crowded elevator
No one knows who farted
And it's like an escalator
One up, one down – we've parted
It's like a burning desire
No one knows what sparked it
It's like a blazing fire
Someone must have started
And it's like an escalator
One up, one down – we've parted
Like a sunny day
The clouds have sorted
The love of your life
A love less courted
And the world's an escalator
Eventually – we're parted

Crowded House of Sin
Won't you let me in
To your crowded house of sin?
I'm just an old man wishing to be young again
The drinks are free
And the powder is flowing
It's my destiny
So that's where I'm going
So either way
You'll see me there
I'll find my way
With a soul to bear
So won't you see to me?
I'm just an old man wishing to be what I used to be

Your Beautiful Font
Life is not what it seems
Or what you want
Yes please write me
With your beautiful font
And I gasp
With every turn of the page
I can't turn away
It cries to me
What I can't see
Everything meant everything
Nothing is free
And I gasp
With every turn of the page
I can't turn away

Lose You

I just want you to feel my pain
So then I'll wash it off in the rain
I just really need your touch
It helps me get through
I just don't want to lose you
I just want to feel my pain
I feel so numb to everything
I just really need this crutch
It helps me get through
I just don't want to lose you
I just want to forget that face
So I'll leave this, memory erased
I just really need your love
It helps me get through
I just don't want to lose you
I just want to make it last
So I'll forget problems from the past
I just really need this crutch
It helps me get through
I just don't want to lose you
But who's for sure what we can endure?
I just don't want to lose you

River of Soul
Follow me down
Waterhole
Follow me down
In a soul
Follow me down
She's got the soul
In her heart
She's got the soul
She's every part
She's got the soul
I could tell you secrets I know
I could show you how the river flows
I could show you all that remains
I could give you a name
Earth wind, love struck
Arrow shot
Earth wind, love struck
All the time
Earth wind, love struck
Sun blaze, love stroke
Everything
Sun blaze, love stroke
All the year
Sun blaze, love stroke
I could tell you secrets I know
I could show you how the river flows
I could show you all that remains
I could give you a name
I don't regret
Any soul I get
I don't regret
Taking...
I don't regret
Any soul I let
Take me
I can tell you secrets of the river
Where it flows and all that remains
I can give you a name

If You Want Me To Leave
If you want me to leave all I blame is me
But I know you don't mean it so please don't say those things
If you want me to stay, what would you want me to say?
Would it be all the things that I remembered to say too late?
If you want me to leave all I blame is me
But I know you don't want that so just come down and see me
If you want me to stay, what would I say?
Would it be all the things that got in the way?

Check Your Head
I knew a psycho barber
He liked to shave too close
Down to the skull he pushed harder
He enjoyed the smell the most
I knew a psycho barber and this is what he said:
Check your head
I knew a voodoo gypsy
She was a call girl too
She didn't care about me
But she wanted you
I knew a voodoo call girl and this is what she said:
Check your head

I'm Sorry
Whenever I feel I've found the answers
I'm talking to myself, there's no one else
Whenever I feel I'm almost home
A sharp u-turn sends me away
So much to say, so much to do
I can't believe I walked out on you
So much to do, so much to say
I just turned and walked away
Whenever I'd feel so winded
You've saved me from myself again
Whenever I feel I'm out of place
You were there to take me away
So much to say, so much to do
I can't believe I walked out on you
So much to do, so much to say
I just turned and walked away
And I'm sorry
I'm sorry
Whenever I'm in deep
Can't believe you're still here for me
So much to say, so much to do
I can't believe I walked out on you
So much to do, so much to say
I just turned and walked away
And I'm sorry
I'm sorry

The Butchers of the World
Don't stop the waves
Don't stop the waves from crashing
Don't stop the blades
Don't stop the blades from slashing
Cut you down
The butchers of the world are gonna cut you down
Don't stop the girl
Don't stop the girl from crying
Don't stop the world
Don't stop the world from dying
Cut you down
The butchers of the world are gonna cut you down
We all drown
We all drown

Prison Prism
I don't think I like this prison
In this little box I'm livin'
While they sit & read my thoughts
Plagiarizing the wars I've fought
And I can't really tell them truths
But I can always sell my ruse
I'll never see the light of day
Until I escape & get away

Superstition
Why can't I vent
Everything I regret?
Can't unwind
Why do I have to make all these problems in my mind?
So infectious, obnoxious
Revelations reveal my superstition
Why can't I sleep?
Away every dream of grief?
Can't let go
Why do I have to deal with people who won't let me flow?
Infections, obnoxious
Revelations reveal my superstition
But you don't listen

Cauterize Me
What about the times we've wasted?
What about the things we said?
What about the times we've wasted on those very words we said?
I cannot break you down
I cannot break you in
I will not throw you out
You are already in
My heart
What about the dreams we had?
Did they all die out like fads?
Failure rests upon the tear soaked clad
I cannot break you down
I cannot break you in
I will not throw you out
You are already in
My heart
Never planned to fall in love so
Everything just told me not to
Can't believe I let you say these things
These words will never cauterize me
Cauterize me
I cannot break you down
I cannot break you in
I will not throw you out
You are already in
You are already in
You're in my heart

Hangman
Up on a hill
With no one else around
I ask still
Where can my answers be found?
I'd wait all day
But I don't have much time to waste
So I guess I'll be seeing you around
Hey, Hangman, do you have the answers?
Hey, Hangman, do you have the answers?
Out in a field
Below stars that fall
How does it feel
To not be involved?
I'd wait all day
But I don't have much time to waste
So I guess I'll wait until you fall
Hey, Hangman, do you have the answers?
Hey, Hangman, do you have the answers?
Hangman, Hey, Hangman
So he opens his eyes
And then he replies
"I've seen too many suns
I've walked too many plains
Tell you no lie, I'd do it again
The answer's in you all, the eyes of the beholders
Whether the mind clouds or even smolders"
Thank you, Hangman

Another Pig in the Mud
As I stand outside this pit - society
There's another pig in the mud for me to see
You hate your lover, you despise your mother
All this pain - I just can't believe
Life is just too hard - I need some relief
The blood running from my arm is getting colder
Colder than before
Hung by their ankles - the victims dangle
And I snort at them as another pig in the mud

The Last Meal
I awaken on a plate
A garnish as my neighbor
I've been chosen and it's time
O, Master, bathe me in spit
Cut me, crush me, take me in
Have me swim through your vomit
Crawling through your entrails
Picking through your shit
Was I the meal you dreamed of?

Goodbye

In a phone call
She comes to you with open arms
You shove her away
With shoulders of cold
A reminder of the days of old
She tells you she still cares
But you fill her head with meaningless scares
No reason to love you
No reason to care
As she soon found out
You'll never be there
All she wanted was your love
To inform you of
Everything in life, just to keep in touch
Sure you said some things, but it wasn't much
Obviously wasn't enough
But enough to make her cry
For what reason was this
Did she make your dreams die?
Another day of haunting
Another day of grief
Another day of wondering why the tears are on her sleeve
A simple open hand
A brutal slap command
The let-go
A final goodbye

Thornless Rose
You're the most beautiful woman I've ever seen
You're one of the smartest people I've ever met
Your heart could not possibly get any bigger, you're so sweet
Your hope is endless and your support for me knows no bounds
Your love is strong
When it's not being held back, your love makes me feel invincible
I'd take a life for you
I'd make a life for you
I'd die for you
I'll never leave
I'll stay with you until my last breath on this earth, and beyond
You're a brat as I'm a jerk
You're hyper-critical as I'm overly insecure
You're a pain in the ass as I, as well, am quite difficult
We've laughed together
We've cried together
We've hurt each other
We've helped each other
We're passionate about everything from our fights to our love making
So here's to you, my thornless rose, for bringing some beauty into my ugly life
I'm eternally grateful and just hope that some day you see what an effect you and your love have had on me

My Kiss
My kiss isn't fair
I use it against her
When her claws come out and her barbs come at me
My lips are my shield and sword
My kiss is a warning
That it indeed may be the last
For if my presence is no longer requested and my leave is required
My lips will give her a history of our emotions in one solitary kiss
My kiss is an outburst
Sexually grasping at straws so she won't feel how scared I am
I hide behind my lips and countless apologies
Afraid of the end I try to avoid with kisses
My kiss...
Isn't a kiss without her

Real
There's so much I wish I could do
I don't know where to start
So much anger that I threw
I feel it coming apart
Whenever I feel like I can't deal
I start to reflect on what is real
And it's love
And it's us

ABOUT THE POET

Christopher Michael Carter was born on May 3rd, 1984 in St. Louis, Missouri. His previous poetry includes *Gun Control for Polar Bears* and his first science fiction novel, *Last Rites of the Capacitance*, is in prepublication. Christopher and his family currently reside in Bevier, Missouri.

www.ingramcontent.com/pod-product-compliance
Lightning Source LLC
Chambersburg PA
CBHW071521080526
44588CB00011B/1515